HOCKEY BASICS

HOCKEY BASICS

by **Norman MacLean**

Introduction by
Emile Francis
President, Hartford Whalers

Illustrated by **Bill Gow**

Photographs by **Con Roach**

Created and Produced by
Arvid Knudsen

PRENTICE-HALL, Inc.
Englewood Cliffs, New Jersey

Dedication

To Norman Alejandro, whose talents
appear to be greater in baseball than in hockey.

Acknowledgement: Our many thanks to the boys,
Alexander Roche, Theseus Roach, Chris Greene and Gregg MacAndrew
for their participation in the photographs in this book.

Other **Sports Basics Books** in Series

Text Copyright © 1983 by Norman MacLean and
Arvid Knudsen

Illustrations and photographs © 1983 by
Arvid Knudsen

All rights reserved. No part of this book may be
reproduced in any form or by any means, except for
the inclusion of brief quotations in a review, without
permission in writing from the publisher.

Book Design by Arvid Knudsen

Printed in the United States of America   -J

Prentice-Hall International, Inc., London
Prentice-Hall of Australia, Pty. Ltd., Sydney
Prentice-Hall Canada, Inc., Toronto
Prentice-Hall of India Private Ltd., New Delhi
Prentice-Hall of Japan, Inc., Tokyo
Prentice-Hall of Southeast Asia Pte. Ltd., Singapore
Whitehall Books Limited, Wellington, New Zealand
Editora Prentice-Hall Do Brasil LTDA., Rio de Janeiro

10 9 8 7 6 5 4 3 2

Library of Congress Cataloging in Publication Data

MacLean, Norman.
  Hockey basics.

  (Sports basics books)
  Includes index.
  Summary: An introduction to the game of ice hockey
including history, equipment, how to play each
position and where to play.
  1. Hockey--United States. 2. Hockey. I. Gow, Bill.
II. Title III. Series.
GV848.4.U6M33 1983   796.9'62   83-9451
ISBN 0-13-392506-4

CONTENTS

INTRODUCTION

by **Emile Francis**
President, *Hartford Whalers*
Member, *Hockey Hall of Fame*

I think hockey is the greatest game in the world and I am thankful that I have been able to participate in it from my early days in North Battleford, Saskatchewan. While General Manager of the New York Rangers, I started the Metropolitan Junior Hockey Association which now has 13 teams in it from Virginia to Eastern Long Island. Eleven players from the association have made it to the National Hockey League and over 300 to college hockey teams.

In St. Louis, where I was president of and general manager of the Blues, I started the Greater St. Louis Junior League. I have always believed in giving back something to the sport that has been so good to me.

The best thing about hockey is that it can be played by almost any youngster. But hockey is in reality two games: The first is skating and the second is stickhandling, checking, and shooting, which creates the super-fast play action.

Learn to skate as early as possible and then play as often as possible—on the frozen pond near your home or in the organized Pee Wee league in your area's ice skating rink. You will feel exhilarated after a day's fun at the pond or rink.

Norman MacLean's Hockey Basics *is just the right introduction to this exciting game. In it he provides the essential elements that you need to learn and understand the sport. He knows—he played hockey, has coached young players, is actively involved in junior youth leagues, and makes his livelihood as a writer/reporter of professional hockey.*

7

The proper hockey stick size for play.

Kingston, Ontario, adherents claim that Britist soldiers stationed in that Canadian city played the first game of hockey in 1855. It was called shinny on ice and used a rubber ball.

THE HISTORY OF HOCKEY / 1

Hockey has its roots in a number of games that were popular in countries other than Canada. The Greeks played their version of field hockey in 550 B.C. In the seventeenth century an ice game known as *kolven* evolved in Holland.

French explorers visiting the St. Lawrence River Valley in 1740 reported coming upon a band of Algonquin Indians playing a combination of lacrosse and hockey on the river and calling out "Ho-gee" whenever a misdirected blow from one of the curved sticks struck an unprotected body.

There is complete justification, however, that hockey on ice, as it is now played, is a Canadian development. The first game probably was played in Montreal on March 3, 1875, when students at McGill University set up rules based on lacrosse, adapted them to the local natural ice skating rink, and played the first game at the Victoria Skating Rink.

Once formal rules were organized, ice hockey mushroomed in popularity. Lord Stanley, the Governour General of Canada, donated the Stanley Cup, now North America's oldest professional sports trophy, to the best amateur team in 1893.

The following year a team from Montreal won the first competition for the Stanley Cup. The year 1893 is also important because the first organized ice hockey game was played in the United States, between Yale University in New Haven, Connecticut, and Johns Hopkins University in Baltimore, Maryland.

Amateur competition for the Stanley Cup continued until the formation in 1910 of the National Hockey Association and the Pacific Coast

Crossover start

Hockey Association. The winners of these two leagues played for the Stanley Cup until the formation of the National Hockey League in 1917.

Hockey was played almost completely outdoors until the Patrick brothers, Frank and Lester, built two artificial rinks in Victoria and Vancouver, British Columbia, in 1912.

The NHL came into complete control of the Stanley Cup when the PCHA folded in 1924, and the players in the Western Canada Hockey League were sold to investors in the United States.

Professional hockey expanded south of the border into the United States, with the Boston Bruins becoming the first American franchise in 1924. The next season saw the last East-West series.

The six-team NHL of the forties, fifties, and sixties was perhaps the most professional of all major leagues in caliber of play—and in profitability. It played to almost 92 percent capacity in the early sixties, bringing on expansion and doubling the league to 12 teams in 1967–68.

In 1972 the fledgling World Hockey Association challenged the NHL as a major league when superstar left wing Bobby Hull of Chicago signed with the Winnipeg Jets. In 1978–79 the WHA folded, and their four teams were taken into the NHL as expansion teams. Today the NHL has 21 teams, 14 in the United States, and 7 in Canada.

The Montreal Canadiens have been the "Yankees" of ice hockey, with 21 Stanley Cup wins since 1915, followed by the Toronto Maple Leafs with 11 playoff titles.

International hockey boomed in 1972 when the first Soviet Union summit series with Canada resulted in a four games to three with one tie win for Canada. Paul Henderson scored three straight winning goals in the final three games played in Moscow, to give Canada the verdict.

The Soviets have won 20 Olympic and World Tourney titles since they won the Gold for the first time at Stockholm in 1954. But the United States captured the Gold in the Olympics at Squaw Valley, California, in 1960, in an upset just as big as their 1980 triumph. Canada hasn't won a World title since 1961, although they did win the 1982 World Junior tournament.

Hockey is a fascinating spectator sport, attracting full-house audiences to the professional arenas in most major cities where the game is played. People love the speed and fierce competition, and the talented, colorful players that make up the game.

Today hockey is played by youngsters from the age of six and up, throughout Europe, the United States, and of course Canada. It is a well-organized sport, attracting hundreds of thousands of kids to teams in leagues guided by official regulations and dedicated coaches and administrators.

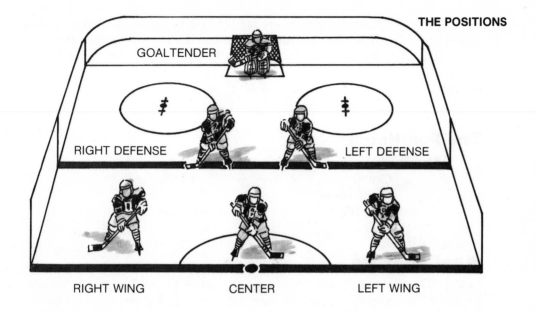

GOALTENDER

RIGHT DEFENSE   LEFT DEFENSE

RIGHT WING   CENTER   LEFT WING

THE OBJECT
OF THE GAME / 2

Scoring more goals than the opposition is the object of the game of ice hockey. A goal is scored when the puck crosses the opposition's goal line inside the posts of the goal net. A goal counts for *one* point.

If the entire puck crosses the goal line it's a goal

1. unless an attacking player kicks the puck into the net or throws or otherwise deliberately directs the puck into the goal by any other means than his stick;

2. unless an attacking player is in the goal crease and is in no way held by a defender while a teammate scores.

Although a goal does not count if kicked in by an attacker, if the same attacker kicks it in off a defender or the goalkeeper, it does count. If a shot deflects off a teammate, the teammate gets credit for the goal and the shooter gets an assist.

11

No more than two assists are credited on any goal, and those assists go to the two players who immediately handled the puck preceding the goal.

The game begins with a face-off in the middle circle of the rink. The referee drops the puck between the center of each team who face each other for the start of play.

The Positions:

The six-player team consists of the

Center	Right Defense
Right Wing	Left Defense
Left Wing	Goaltender

What They Do

Center: The center operates mostly up and down the middle of the ice and usually leads his team's attack by carrying the puck. He sets up plays by exchanging passes with his two wing-men and tries to steer the play in toward the opponent's goal. Defensively, he tries to keep the play in the attacking zone by harassing the opponent's puck carrier (forechecking). After the opposition works the puck out of their end of the rink, he tries to interrupt their playmaking as the puck moves through the neutral zone and into his defending zone (backchecking).

Wings: The two wings move up and down the sides of the rink with the direction of play. Offensively, they skate abreast of the center, exchanging passes with him while positioning themselves for a shot on the goal. Defensively, they watch the opponent's wings and try to disrupt their playmaking and shooting as the action moves back toward the defending zone (backchecking).

Defensemen: Basically, the two defensemen try to stop the incoming play at their own blue line. They also block shots, clear the puck from in front of their goal, and watch the opposing forwards. Offensively, they carry the puck up the ice or pass the puck up to the forwards, then follow the play into the attacking zone and help to keep it there.

Goalkeeper: The goalkeeper's main responsibility is to keep the puck from entering the goal, and there are no restrictions placed on the methods he can employ. His offensive contributions are limited and consist of occasionally passing the puck up to his defensemen or forwards to start a rush. A goalkeeper almost never scores a goal and only on rare occasions does he receive credit for an assist.

The Rink

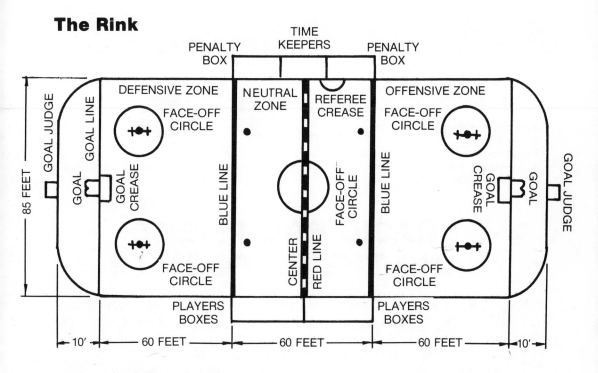

How to Join a Team

The Amateur Hockey Association of the United States has 11,000 teams registered in what might be the most organized amateur sport in the United States. That means there are approximately 165,000 players. In addition, those players are served by 8,000 coaches and 8,000 referees.

To join a team go to your nearest skating rink. Almost all rinks run "house" leagues that have AHAUS programs.

In the eight-to-twelve-year-old bracket there are three age breakdowns. Mites must be eight years of age or younger by December 31 of the current playing season. Squirts must be ten years of age or younger by December 31 of the current season, and Pee Wees, 12 or younger by December 31 of the current season.

Just as baseball has the more advanced Babe Ruth League, young players can identify with their elders in the Bantams (14 or younger), Midgets (16 or younger) and Juniors (19 or younger).

Once you get on a team you will receive coaching through AHAUS clinics and the Coaching Achievement Program. An early start in skating helps a player to make the team. After that, playing the game of ice hockey is fun.

13

Skates

They are the most important equipment you will own. They come in three different types for hockey. The shoe part should be of strong leather, fit perfectly, and have a strong arch support, or counter, of reinforced material. Buy them from a store specializing in skates.

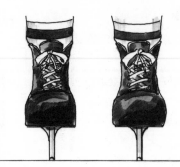

Each blade of the skate has a hollow throughout its length. The inside of the hollow is the "inside" edge, the outside is the "outside" edge.

BASIC EQUIPMENT AND THE UNIFORM / 3

The cost of equipping even a young boy for hockey has escalated. In the early eighties, sales tags at Gerry Cosby & Co. of New York, outfitters to more than a dozen NHL teams, showed the following:

Skates: From $30 to $115 for a junior pro model.

Helmets: $8 to $40.

Masks: $15 to $25.

Gloves: $15 to $80.

Shin guards: $10 to $60.

Elbow pads: $10 to $50.

Cup and supporter: $6.

Suspenders: $6.

Garter belt: $8.

Stockings: $10.

Pants: $15 to $75.

Jersey: $10 to $150. (The $150 jersey is an exact NHL replica.)

Sticks: $5 to $20.

Goalie sticks: $10 to $30.

Goalie pads: $30 to $500. ($500 is Pro replica.)

Gloves: $25 to $250.

Cups: $20.

Chest protector: $15 to $50.

Shoulder and arm pads: $15 to $75.

Forward's skate   Defensemen's skate   Goalie's skate

Protective Equipment
and the Uniform

The Helmet
One-piece helmets are acceptable, although a two-piece helmet adjusts better. They can be of leather or plastic.

Face Guard and Mouth Guard
Most junior and youth hockey leagues require the wearing of face masks that are made of plastic.

The Stick
Made of wood of northern ash or rock elm or plastic, the sticks are made in left, right, or neutral lies. Most boys will use lie #5 or #6. A low lie (#3 or #4) puts the blade, and therefore the puck, farthest from the feet. A high lie (#7) brings the blade and the puck closer to the players' feet.

Taping
The stick should be taped from heel to toe with a nob of tape formed at the top of the shaft. It keeps the puck from sliding off the stick.

Gloves
Gauntlet style heavy leather gloves with padding and extension should be of good quality and flexible.

Pants, Waist, Spine, and Kidney Pads
Shock-absorbing inner padding is sewn in waist, spine, and hip areas of the short pants. Thigh pads are also sewn in.

Shoulder Harness
Shoulder pads should be lightweight and not bulky. The harness, or chest protector, and the biceps pads are made of foam rubber.

Protective Cup
Boys should wear one of these at all times during practice and games.

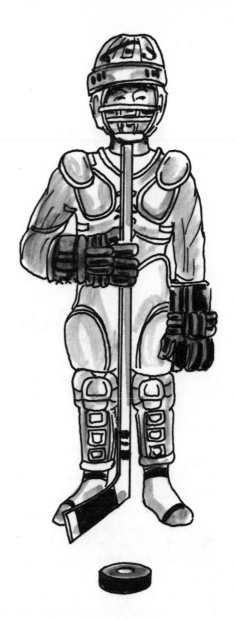

Shin Guards and Knee Caps
They are made of hard leather or plastic held on by light elastic. Stockings are held up by a garter belt.

The proper protective equipment is vital in order to play as injury-free as possible.

Left foot skating forward
on the inside edge.

Left foot skating forward
on the outside edge.

SKATING / 4

Skating is the most important skill in hockey. If you cannot skate, you cannot play—it's that simple. Skating must be almost as automatic as walking in order to play at any decent level of competitive ice hockey.

Hard work and proper fitting skate boots are important for learning how to skate.

Sometimes skating style is determined by the physical build of the skater: Tall skaters have longer strides; shorter skaters, little choppy strides. But there are exceptions. Learning to skate at an early age helps to make skating automatic.

It is vital to learn to stop or turn in either direction. Usually when you start, your first few strides are short running steps designed to pick up speed. To start, the skater leans forward and more or less throws himself in the direction he wishes to go. In stopping, the player must simply put most of his weight on the outside of his foot and turn the blades of his skates parallel.

It is important that you learn to skate in both directions by skating both clockwise and counterclockwise. At most rinks three quarters of skating time is clockwise, and it takes an effort to learn the reverse.

Stops and starts help both skating skill and conditioning. A good skating drill is to circle the entire rink in a huge figure eight while circling both nets. Always "cross over" when turning, do not glide around turns. Most young players find it easier to cross the right foot over the left but have difficulty in crossing the left over the right.

Forward crossover sequence

Carry your hockey stick when you skate unless forbidden to do so by the rink you are practicing on. It is important to coordinate the movement of your stick with your body as you skate.

Also, check your blades before play or practice—they may need sharpening. This will give you a better edge. Sharpening is a must before a game.

Quick Starts: In order to play hockey, you must be able to stop and start almost instantaneously and go in whatever direction is indicated by the play.

To start quickly from a stop position thrust your left foot forward and bend your left knee at the same time. Push off with your left skate by angling the skate slightly to the left on the ice so that you have a pushing surface. You must start from a slight crouch, slightly bending forward from the waist. Push hard on the turned left leg, then straighten your leg.

Now do exactly the same thing with your right foot. Bend forward and push off on the ice. By alternating this way between your right and left feet, you will slowly pick up speed. Usually the first few steps are short choppy ones; then as speed increases, your strides become longer.

Stop and start sequence going in same direction

Skating Speed: In order to fly up the ice, you simply push with one foot and glide with the other. Skating rhythm is everything. The proper coordination of all parts of the body—feet, hips, knees, and shoulders—produces that fluid overdrive, or glide, that is pleasureable. After you get it right, it will seem easy.

Remember when gliding to keep your upper body ahead of your hips. This will help your balance. You must master rhythm or you will forever use choppy strides. The length of your stride is determined by you and what feels best for you.

How to Stop: When the play reverses and goes in the opposite direction in an instant, everyone on the ice must stop, turn, and go in the other direction in order not to be "trapped" out of the play.

Stop and start sequence going in opposite direction

The prescribed method of stopping is to turn your hips and skate blades parallel across the line of direction you are skating. If you turn your skates until they are at right angles to your direction and then "dig" the inside edge of your blades into the ice, you will stop at once. Since most hockey stops are made to change direction, bend one knee forward a bit as you stop, and then start the push-off motion needed for a quick start.

Turning: In skating you must be able to turn in either direction. The glide-around turn is extremely easy. If you wish to perform a glide, turn to the left and turn your head and the upper part of your body to the left. Lean a bit inward and bend your left knee. Without too much effort you will glide to the left.

But in hockey, turns are usually much sharper in their angle than glides and must be made at fairly high speeds. As a result, when turning you must "cross over" on each alternate stride. When turning left, you will cross the right foot over in front of the left and "lean" and "push off" in the direction of the turn. The reverse is true when turning right. The more forcefully you push off after crossing over, the faster you will start in the reverse direction—and perhaps the quicker you will get to the puck.

Skating Backwards: Everyone, not just defensemen, must be able to skate backward. You do exactly the same thing you do when skating forward except that you "sit down" in your pants and lean your backside in the backward direction you are skating.

Here are two drills:

1. Skate backward the entire length of the rink, lifting first one skate and then the other completely off the ice.
2. Skating backward, stop at every line, turning left at the first line and right at the next.

Straight backward start

When skating backward you should "hang" your chest forward in order to maintain balance. Always lift your skates from the ice and push off, don't glide.

Power-Skating

Power-skating is a fancy term for using the edges of your skate blades, basing all of your movements on the principle of inside and outside edging. Along with this simple concept is the idea of a basic stance, with the knees bent slightly more than the average hockey player is used to, but if perfected will give almost perfect balance on skates.

Each skate blade (defensemen, forwards, and goalies all use slightly different skates) has a hollow running its entire length. The inside of this hollow is called the inner edge, and the outside is called the outer edge.

The Long Exercise: Always get into a good hockey position to start power drills. Now push off with either skate to the side, keeping your weight on the ball of the foot. Extend the leg to the fullest, with the skate as close to the ice as possible at the end of the thrust. Then bring the leg back to its original position by executing a letter *C* backward. Bring the foot forward and glide for a count of two. The feet should be a shoulder width apart during the glide.

The Stride: The stride is the same as the long exercise, except that you don't glide for the count of two but push off again immediately, guaranteeing more speed. Thrust to the side, with your weight evenly balanced, knees

19

Forward stride sequence and release

bent, upper body stationary, and head up. Remember that it is not possible to begin the thrust unless both feet are on the ice at the start.

Therefore, when a thrust is completed, make sure your weight is returned completely to the returned foot before beginning the next thrust.

Two Feet Forward Inside Edges: Hold your stick in front of you at shoulder height. Do not raise your skates from the ice during this drill. Remember to bend your knees, head up, feet a shoulder width apart. Now turn your toes out, pressing on your inside edges. Then turn your toes in, your skates completing semicircles. After toeing in, snap your skates back to their original position while applying your weight to the back of your skates without lifting the blades.

Forward Half Inside Edges: This drill is the same as the previous one except the skater turns or thrusts on one blade at a time rather than both. For greater balance keep the foot not thrusting on a slight inside edge.

Forward Inside Edges—One Foot: Skate two or three strides, then at a command push off with the right inside edge. Raise the right foot and attach it to the left skating boot. This gives balance and stability.

Forward Outside Edges—One Foot: Skate two or three strides and then, on command, lift your right skate slightly and cross it in front of your left skate, putting the blade down on the right outside edge. Then thrust with your left outside edge. If you complete this, you will form an outside semicircle.

There are many other combinations, such as switching from inside to outside edges while skating forward, a three-hundred-and-sixty-degree turn, skating from backward to forward in the same direction, and rink turns using the outside edges. Later as your skating improves there will be other combinations and crossovers and forward crossovers.

Ultimately you will skate backward. The same drills are used except you are skating backward.

Back Inside Edges—Two Feet: With your feet no more than a shoulder width apart, toe both feet in. Your feet will complete two half circles. When you return your skates to their original position, bring your heels together, then straighten the feet into the starting position. Remember not to let your heels come up off the ice.

A back crossover is simple, but must be done perfectly. Right skate pushes, then cross over left, while left thrusts back. Now the player pauses as if analyzing his opponent's next move, and then does another crossover but leads with the left skate (on both inside edges for balance). Leading with the left skate moves him to the opposite side while still skating backward.

Backing in

There are two things to guard against. If a player while executing a back crossover slides the lead foot over the thrusting foot instead of picking it up, the distribution of the weight is uncertain. When it is picked up and crossed over, the weight is on the back foot as it should be. Not thrusting properly in your haste to get to the puck in a game can actually cost a player speed. In backward crossovers remember to thrust properly with the back foot.

The days when a coach simply threw the puck on the ice and let every-one scrimmage while learning to skate on their own are over. In order to play hockey you must spend lots of time skating with guidance.

Ready for action

YOUR PHYSICAL CONDITION / 5

Physical conditioning, or being in top shape, can make the difference between the average player and the good one. An outstanding, talented player who is not in shape will always lose out to an average player who comes ready to play, both mentally and physically.

Sleep: You must keep fit all year round, not just during the season. A young athlete in the years between eight and 13 needs more sleep than the average person, perhaps between seven and nine hours a night. And a nap of three to five hours before a game, if possible, is also recommended.

Exercises: Hockey's best conditioner is still skating, but dry land exercises in the off season and prior to training camp have become popular. Skipping rope tones your legs, and certain other gymnastic-type exercises are of value. Running on your skates develops drive and power, as does running in the sand on the beach in the summertime.

Food: Eat well-balanced meals with medium amounts of liquid. During a game or workout, do not drink soda pop or carbonated beverages. It is a safe practice to eat a hot meal and drink a glass of milk four hours or more before a game or scrimmage in order to avoid a sluggish feeling while playing. A hot dog and a soda just before game time is not recommended.

You must learn to carry the puck with your stick

THE BASIC SKILLS
YOU NEED TO PLAY / 6

Holding Your Stick

In hockey 75 percent of all players shoot left-handed. Over the years, right-handed-shooting right wings have dominated the NHL: Gordie Howe, Andy Bathgate, and Mike Bossy. Many European players play the off-wing: that is, they play right wing while shooting left.

But the important thing is a proper grip and control of the stick. The top hand must control and guide your stick with a firm grip. Your wrist coordinates inward with your thumb at the back of the shaft. By keeping the thumb at the back of the shaft, you keep the blade of the stick closed. This will give you a strong, accurate shot or pass.

If you're right-handed, your lower hand should be your right hand and the reverse if you're left-handed. The lower hand moves up and down the stick. It is the power hand, with the stick held completely in your fingers and the thumb over the shaft. Control of the puck depends completely upon your grip. A loose top hand will misdirect your shots.

Stickhandling: To play hockey you must learn to dribble the puck or carry it with your stick. When you carry the puck forward, you cup the puck in the middle of your stick and advance it with soft side-to-side sweeps, varying the sweeps in width. Remember to toe in your stick blade while tilting it slightly over the puck to maintain control.

Now comes the hard part: Just as a basketball player dribbles up court while looking at his opponents, a hockey player must keep his head up while carrying the puck. When learning, glance down once in a while to see it, but keep your head up most of the time. It is vital to have a full view of your teammates and your opponents.

If you look down at the puck, you will lose passing opportunities to teammates and become prey to opponents who will body check you without warning. Try to always keep two hands on your stick. Most NHL professionals pass without looking down to find the puck, simply by feel. You will develop a sort of split vision, in which you sense where the puck is and still see the other action.

One exercise that is still popular is to place chairs or cones on the ice at intervals of ten feet. Then start behind one net and stickhandle the length of the ice while zigzagging between the chairs or cones. If you look down at the puck, you will eventually bump into a chair or cone.

Protecting the Puck While Carrying It: After learning to carry the puck, you must practice what to do when an opponent challenges you. If you come to a point where an opponent is about a stick's length away from you, pull the puck away from your opponent's stick and shield it with your body.

To "go around" a checker or a defenseman while carrying the puck, move the puck wide to your backhand, as you near your opponent's extended stick. At the same time, skate sharply around him, without letting him know what you are going to do. If you do, he will meet you head on.

Passing

When you watch the fine precision passing of Wayne Gretzky, Jari Kurri, Glenn Anderson on the forward line and point men Paul Coffey and Charley Huddy of the Edmonton Oilers as they work a power play, it seems the puck is tied by an invisible string between their sticks. They seem to be parts of a machine instead of individuals. The secret to this: position play and good passing.

In order to pass with skill, you must be able to pass either on your forehand or backhand and also to receive or "catch" a pass on your stick, either forehanded or backhanded. You must also know *when* to pass.

The mechanics of passing a puck are simple. Cup the puck in the blade of your stick. Do not slap it. Sharp passes are best made when you can keep the puck on the ice. Look where you are passing and "lead" your teammate by a stride or two, so that he doesn't have to break his skating stride to receive your pass.

When receiving a pass, hold the stick hard just as the puck is about to make contact with the blade of your stick. Don't let the puck control or push your stick. Also, bend the stick slightly in the direction of the pass and make a wall to stop the puck. The same goes for receiving a pass on the back hand, though even some NHL pros have a problem with this.

Don't shoot the puck at your teammate, but put enough force behind it so it gets to him without being intercepted; and don't try to pass through a mass of players in your own defensive zone—an interception can lead to a goal by the opposition.

Basically there are five types of passes: the on-the-ice pass, the flip pass, the push pass, the drop pass, and the back pass.

On-the-Ice Pass: This is the most common pass and it can be delivered either forehanded or backhanded. It resembles a shot, but without as much force. The puck remains flat on the ice.

Flip Pass: As your skill increases, you will try to flip the puck over your opponents' sticks to a teammate beyond. A flip pass is elevated ten to twelve inches off the ice and lands a couple of feet in front of the intended receiver. It is best done with a flick of the toe of the blade and is a slow pass. This is the preferred pass when a player is trying to center the puck in front of the goal from behind the opponent's net and the slot area is guarded by a defenseman.

Push Pass: Almost a lost art today, the puck is pushed forward with both hands on the stick in the same motion. The puck will stop almost exactly to the spot where a teammate skates to pick it up.

Drop Pass: The drop pass is employed when a teammate is trailing a puck carrier. The puck carrier simply leaves the puck behind him on the ice, and his teammate skates in and picks it up. It is almost always used in the attacking zone. If a defenseman is skating backward guarding the puck carrier, suddenly he has two men to guard, one of whom may take him out by checking him, after drop-passing to his trailing teammate.

Back Pass: The back pass is often made "blind" to a certain spot where a teammate is supposed to be. It is a flat-on-the-ice pass, and most often serves to pass the puck back to the point on the power play.

Shooting

There are two basic shots in hockey: the wrist shot and the more glamorous slap shot.

You are able to control the puck with the wrist shot. It can be gotten away quicker with an instant flick of the wrist. Quickness in instantly shooting the puck is the key to most goals. And it can be aimed exactly where the shooter wants it to go.

Boomer Geoffrion of the Montreal Canadiens started the slap-shot craze in 1950, and his success and the later success of Bobby Hull, the Chicago Black Hawks Golden Jet who scored 610 NHL goals and 303 more in the World Hockey Association, created a universal desire among young players to slap or golf the puck instead of flicking it.

Wrist Shot: A wrist shot is a simple flick of the wrist after first cradling the puck in the center of the blade. Always look where you are shooting, not at the puck. Aim at a specific spot and flick the wrist *without looking* at the puck.

Slap Shot: Raise your stick on a parallel line to the ice somewhere between the hip and shoulders and hit behind the puck on the ice.

Checking

In order to guard your man, you must know how to poke check, hook check, or body check when he has the puck, and also how to cover a man who does not have the puck.

Poke Check: A poke check is a quick jab, or thrust, with your stick at the puck while releasing your lower stick hand.

Hook Check: To hook-check you bend your body low and reach the length of your stick as far as possible while holding it with only one hand. At the same time, place as much of your stick as possible on the ice. If you play hockey left-handed, stride forward to the right with your right foot at the same time that you make the arch with your stick.

Body-Checking: Body-checking has become less important with the advent of the speedier offensive game of the eighties. Before World War II and before the 1943 introduction of the center red line that speeded up getting the puck out of a team's defensive zone, body-checking was an art. It meant a great deal when carrying the puck was the rule instead of headmanning it (explained later), and the game was slower and more individualistic.

To body-check you push off the rear foot, and as your target nears you, you drive your shoulder and hip into his body. Timing is very important, because if you miss, your opponent will skate around you on his way to your net. Also, you might hurt yourself by crashing into the sideboards. Good body-checkers start to body-check with their knees bent and their skates well apart.

Tips on Checking: When checking while skating backward, defensemen usually extend their sticks as far as possible in front of them and either poke-check or hook-check. If you are left-handed and the attacker swerves left, you poke-check. If he goes right, you hook-check.

OFFENSIVE PLAY / 7

Before the advent of Bobby Orr in 1965, offensive play meant the work of the forward line (center, left wing, and right wing) with occasional help from a good skating defenseman who could assist the three forwards. After Orr hockey changed, and most defensemen tried to emulate him. He created the four-man attack, and ultimately this led to the present five-man ganging attack, especially in power play situations in which the offense has a one-man advantage.

Now skating is a far more paramount skill than in the past. Nonetheless, despite the all-out-attack concepts, much has not changed.

The Center: The main job of the center is to patrol the center lane of the ice and also to handle face-offs. The center is allowed to follow the puck wherever it goes, and he should be a good skater, since his job requires him to carry the puck more than anyone else. His primary function is to feed his wings with scoring passes. This concept was dealt a partial blow by the advent of Phil Esposito in the seventies. A large-sized man, Esposito planted himself in the slot—that area in front of the goal—and received passes from his wings Ken Hodge and Wayne Cashman.

Despite exceptions like Esposito, a center's main function is still to carry the puck and make plays for his wingers and defensemen when they are integrated into the attack.

Left Wing: The left wing patrols an area twenty feet out from the left boards and is responsible for checking the opposition's right wing. He is expected to assist his fellow forwards and defensemen on attack and also to come back and help the defense. His primary function is to score goals.

A wrist shot

Right Wing: The right wing's duties are exactly the same, except he patrols the right lane and guards the opposition's left wing.

Headmanning the Puck: A basic principle of any play is headmanning the puck. That simply means sending it up the ice when you see a teammate is in a position to receive a pass rather than to carry the puck yourself.

If you attempt to stickhandle from one end of the ice to the other, you'll draw a crowd of opponents. This is very dangerous, especially in your own defensive end. When you have the puck in your opponent's zone, you have more leeway.

When to Throw in the Puck: On occasion you will be forced to dump the puck or throw it into your opponent's zone instead of carrying it in because the defense is too strong. This usually occurs when the opposition has more than one forward backchecking in addition to the two defensemen. It has become less common since the success of the 1980 U.S. Olympic team which believed in carrying the puck over the opposition's blue line.

Three-on-Two Attack: Hockey does not have set plays as in football or basketball. Still, certain situations call for certain plays. There is the basic three-on-two, in which the three-man forward line gets the chance to skate in and attack the opponent's two defensemen. Most teams try to isolate one defenseman or one of the three forwards, thus reducing the play to a two-on-one situation for the remaining two forwards.

Two-on-One: In a two-on-one, the puck carrier will try to draw the defenseman to one side. He then gives his teammate a pass and puts him in for a free shot on the goalie. Too much passing is no good; always make sure to get a shot on goal.

The Slot: The ideal spot to shoot from is the twelve-to-eighteen-foot radius in front of the net. The closer you get to the net, the more your angle is cut down. If the goalie comes out of the net, he will cut down the angle still further.

Rebounds and Deflections: Many scoring chances come as a result of rebounds of original shots. A shooter should try to shoot about two inches off the ice, which is the toughest chance for a goalie. The key is to be in the right spot at the right time—in front of the net.

Analyze the Goalie: Now that you have learned how to shoot and are in the right position to do so, remember you still have to beat the goalie. If he moves too soon and slides straight out to meet you, deke (*see Glossary*) him to either the right or left and simply tuck the puck in the net.

If, however, he goes down before you shoot, simply lift the puck over him. If he moves from one side of the net to the other, catch him going the wrong way and put the puck in the opposite side. Test him on backhand shots and on his ability to stop a shot on the ice.

Defensive Duties of the Forward Line: We have already mentioned the men on the opposition that the forward line guards. However, when your opponent has the puck in your defensive zone things change. The right wing guards the left point. He stations himself along the right boards, midway between the goal line and the blue line. This enables him to cover the left point or defenseman at the blue line and still scramble in the corner with the opponent's forwards.

The center's job is to cover the puck no matter where it goes. The left wing's responsibilities are the reverse of the right wing's along the other boards. During the original rush, the left wing handles the opposition's right wing and vice versa until that rush is broken up and the puck is in the zone.

Positional play is important except when desperate measures are needed in case some of your teammates are trapped up-ice and you must do anything to prevent a score by your opponents. If you are in your proper positions, it will help the transition to attack when your team gains possession of the puck.

Killing Penalties: The normal formation in the defensive zone is known as the *box* when a team is one man short. The forwards attempt to cover the point men and sluff off back into the middle or slot area where most goals are scored. When you have cleared the puck down the ice to the other team's end, most teams will follow the formula of sending one forechecker in first, to harass the opposition. This man should be a good skater who always keeps in motion and turns and comes back up-ice with the puck carrier.

The second penalty killer may go in, depending upon the success of the first. Remember to keep in motion when killing a penalty because the opposition has the extra man.

Two Men Short: In two-men-short situations, most teams put their fastest man on ice.

The basic defensive formation is the triangle. This consists of two defensemen in front of the net and one forward at the point of the apex in the slot, trying to guard whichever point man gets the puck.

Face-Offs: A key duty of most centers is taking *face-offs*. In modern hockey, many teams put two centers on the ice during face-offs in their own end, in case one is removed by a lineman during the face.

The two main methods of facing off are a backhand sweep (a sweep of the stick with a backhand motion, with the blade open) or a forehand draw. Watch the puck in the official's hands and react instantly when he drops it.

Tips: A forward who is a puck hog and won't pass is not an asset. A good team player is unselfish. Still, playing up front gives a player a chance to shine individually, if he remembers that teamwork and precision-passing are musts.

Skate to Open Ice: The influx of European players into North American pro hockey and the success of the 1980 U.S. Gold Medal winners at the Lake Placid Olympics has led to a mix of cultures. Herb Brooks, the coach of the New York Rangers and of the U.S. Olympians, preaches a European-style weave attack in which the right wing crosses over to the left and vice versa and offensive players skate to open ice in the attack zone in order to receive passes. This concept, similar to basketball, demands that a player keep in motion without the puck.

Forcing puck carrier wide

DEFENSIVE PLAY / 8

Despite the all-out-attack concept of hockey in the eighties, defensive play still has four main concepts: defending in your own end, breaking out or clearing the puck from your own end, attacking up the ice in concert with the forwards, and defending against breakouts from the other team's end. The last line of defense is the goaltender, who has his own special section, because this position has no similarity to any other phases of hockey.

Defending in Your Own Zone: A defenseman must team up with his defense partner when the other team has the puck. One man covers the front of the net and the other takes the corner. When the puck is in the left corner, the left defenseman should go there, with the right defenseman covering the slot. The reverse is true when the puck goes into the right corner.

Clearing the slot is an art, but a player who wants to body-check opponents there to prevent possible scoring chances must also maintain an awareness of the puck.

A basic rule is that one defenseman should always be in front of the net. You must divide the ice into two zones—right and left—and cover it. A defenseman should always know where the puck is.

Defending Against a Three-on-Two: In the classic three-on-two, the defensemen back-skate with their sticks extended as far as possible in front of them. Their extended sticks may deflect a pass and serve as a delaying action until help in the form of your own backchecking forwards can arrive.

The defenseman not playing the puck carrier plays a little behind his partner and always tries to stay between the net and the forwards on his side. Doug Harvey, a hall-of-Fame defenseman, never worried about the puck. He simply backed up, looked the forward squarely in the eyes, and took his body when he got the opportunity. He played in the NHL until he was 45.

Three-on-One: Back up in the middle and try to snare a bad pass. Also hope for a mistake by the opposition.

Two-on-Two: This is really a man-on-man situation. Play the man, not the puck. Keep your body between him and the goal. If he passes, your partner should help. If possible angle him into a corner, slow him down, and pin him.

Two-on-One: In a dangerous two-on-one situation the lone defenseman takes one forward and the goalie takes the other, usually the puck carrier. The defenseman backs in and tries to intercept any passes.

One-on-One: Simply play man-to-man. Look the puck carrier in the eye and forget the puck, especially if the carrier is a great distance from your goal. Continue to guard the man even after he shoots the puck. The puck is then the goalie's job, not yours.

Don't Back In: There is almost no situation except two-on-ones in which it is not better to stand up on the blue line and meet the oncoming forwards.

Blocking Shots: The art of blocking shots is almost a lost technique because of the speed of the modern game.

When the forward gets too close, go down and block his shot because he has committed himself. Watch the forward's face. Many forwards look down when they shoot, and this is the exact second to go down to block the shot. If you drop when he is close, the shot will hit you on the pads. If you go down too soon, he will deke around you, or worse yet, hit you in the face with the shot.

Face-offs: Defensemen take few face-offs but must align themselves as part of the picket line guarding the goal on face-offs deep in their own zone.

Breaking Out of Your Own End: The instant you get possession look for a forward to break out to whom you can pass or headman the puck to. Some defensemen go behind their net, stop, and look over the ice. Many teams don't believe in this system, because it invites forechecking. *Never* throw the puck away without looking, however, and *if necessary* freeze it against the boards for a face-off rather than giving it away.

Defensemen on Attack: A defenseman's main duty on attack is to man the points. The point, either left or right, is the area just over your opponent's blue line, just inside your attack zone.

BODY CHECKING

The defenseman must stop the puck from coming back into neutral ice. Then he has the choice of passing or shooting on the net.

Try not to shoot into a defense player. If the puck bounces back off him, it can lead to a breakaway for the opposition. If you can't shoot or pass, throw the puck back into the corner and keep the attack in motion.

Leading a Rush: Defensemen may lead an attacking rush. The chance to attack may happen by a quick break or by blocking a shot which bounces in front of you and enables you to reverse the direction of play and get a jump on your opponents. The forward who takes your place on defense should follow up and take your position on the point.

THE GOALTENDER / 9

The goaltender can be as much as ninety percent responsible for the winning or losing of a hockey game. A team can outplay its opponent territorially, but lose because they can't beat the padded man in front of the cage. Similarly, a goalie can have a bad night despite few shots on goal and cost his team the game.

Sticks: A goalie's stick cannot exceed three and one half inches, except at the heel of the blade, where it may not exceed four and one half inches. The wide section of the stick cannot extend more than 26 inches up the shaft. Most goalies use a lie 12 or 13 stick. A higher stick lie is used by a stand-up goalie who wants to handle the puck.

Gloves: Goalies use a catching mitt similar to a first baseman's trapper.

Chest Protectors: Hockey chest protectors resemble a baseball catcher's chest protector. They should be about one and a half inches thick and must not restrict movement. Most goalies wear regular hockey pants with the charley horse pads removed and felt padding substituted.

Masks: Today all goalies wear masks. Some of them even decorate their masks with all sorts of fancy paint jobs so they resemble the prows of ships, apparently in the hope of frightening shooters. Masks are made of fiberglass and have ear, eye, nose, and mouth slits. However, most youth hockey goaltenders use bird-cage-type masks, similar to a catcher's mask.

Modern-day NHL goalkeepers subject themselves to being the targets for pucks that are fired at up to 95 mph, as their team's last line of defense. When his teammates have the puck up at the other end of the rink, he may relax, but when it gets to center ice, he must adopt the "ready" position. His feet should be wide enough apart to keep the pads closed. The goalie bends at the waist, bringing his eyes closer to the ice. He must always watch the puck. Another must is to keep the stick flat on the ice in front of the skates.

A glove save

The stick should be held in the upper hand at the bottom of the narrow part of the shaft. The knees should be bent enough so he can move in any direction. His catching hand open, ready to catch the puck, and his eyes should never leave the puck.

The stick is used to stop ice-level shots, the pads to block those shots moderately high, with the stick and catching hand ready to cover one side of the net. The other side is the "far side" which usually gives a shooter a tiny opening just big enough for a shooter to aim at. The blades of the skates are the prescribed method to kick out shots on the ice to the far side.

Breakaways: The goaltender should wait for the shooter to make the first move. If possible, the shooter should be decoyed with a stick or head feint into moving first.

Pass-Outs: A goalie must use his stick to bat the puck away on pass-outs from behind the net or the corners. Also, the stick is used to bat rebounds into the corners or drop down and smother them if necessary.

On-the-Ice Shots: In stopping and kicking out on-the-ice shots, the skate blade turns outward so the puck will deflect to the side boards. The same technique should be used when making a stick-save with an on-the-ice shot.

Screen Shots: The screen shot is the toughest shot a goalie has to stop, except for deflections in which luck plays a big part. Many goalers get scored upon without seeing the puck, but if they are in the right spot, they sometimes stop the puck by simply being hit by it. Also, by playing in a crouch the goalie may spot the puck through the maze of sticks, legs, and skates out there.

Catching the Puck: If the goalie can catch the puck, he should do so, because he can then control it. There will be no rebound and he can then throw the puck behind the goal line to a teammate.

Tip-ins and Deflections: Hope and quick reflexes are the only way to stop these goals. In the past they were almost accidents, but now each team has a slot specialist who is adept at changing the course of the puck when it is about ten feet from the goalie.

Almost all coaches prefer a goalie who stands up. Although many professionals drop down, young goalies should learn to stand up. The cardinal sin of goaltending is to go down before the shooter shoots. With a deke, the forward then has a half-empty net to shoot at.

Playing the Angles: When the puck carrier seems to be ready to shoot, the goalie should station himself at the front of the crease in relation to the shooter and reduce the shooting angle to each corner. If the puck carrier fakes a shot and moves laterally, the goalie should keep his eyes on the puck and move with the puck, not the player.

Face-offs: The goalie should always be ready for a direct shot on the net from the face-off. Mostly, however, the attack tries to get the puck back to a shooter at the point, so the goalie should swing slightly in his direction.

Coming Out of the Net: When Jacques Plante left his net and stopped loose pucks that were coming around in back of his goal, with the result that his defensemen got the puck instead of its traveling around the boards where opposing forwards could contest for it, it was considered quite daring. Now 25 years later it is routine. This is a simple technique for the goalie to gain possession for his team.

PENALTIES ARE PART OF THE GAME / 10

The referee is the absolute boss in a hockey game. He can be helped by linemen and goal judges, but he has the final decision on all aspects of play.

Infractions of the rules are signaled to the players and the spectators by the referee. Most of the penalties will cause a team to play shorthanded for two minutes. Stiffer penalties can be called. The common penalties and signals are:

Holding: Intentionally holding an opponent in any manner (2 min.).

Hooking: Using a stick as a body "hook" to impede an opponent (2 min.).

Interference: Obstructing an opponent who doesn't have the puck (2 min.).

Tripping: Pulling an opponent down with a stick, knee, foot, arm, or hand (2 min.).

High-Sticking: Carrying a stick above the shoulder into or close to an opponent (2 or 5 min.).

Slashing: Swatting an opponent with the stick (2 or 5 min.).

Misconduct: Abusive language to an official (10 min., team not short on ice).

Slow Whistle: Signal indicating that the referee will call a penalty once the offending team controls the puck.

Charging: Taking 2 or more strides before hitting opponent (2 or 5 min.).

Icing: Signal used by a linesman.

Cross-Checking: Holding stick with both hands and pushing handle into opponent (2 or 5 min.).

Elbowing: Directing elbow into opponent (2 or 5 min.).

Washout: When used by a referee, it means goal disallowed. When used by a linesman, it means there is no icing or no offside.

Bench Penalty: Assessed for abusive language or other breach of conduct at the bench (2 min.).

Boarding: Violently checking a puck carrier into the boards (2 or 5 min.).

Broken Stick: Assessed on a player using a broken stick (2 min.).

Butt-Ending: Jabbing the butt end of the stick into an opponent (5 min.).

Delay of Game: Any deliberate attempt to delay the game (2 min.).

Fighting: Fisticuffs (1 or 2 two-min. penalties, or 5 min.).

Kneeing: Driving a knee into an opponent (2 or 5 min.).

Match Penalty: For deliberate injury or attempt to injure (5 or 10 min. with no right of replacement or ejection).

Penalty Shot: Awarded to player who is pulled down from behind on a clear breakaway or when defensive player other than goalie falls on the puck in the crease. An offensive player is allowed to skate in alone on the goalie in a penalty shot.

Playing with Illegal Stick: (Called on protest by opponent). Stick is measured. If illegal, player penalized (2 min.). If legal, protesting team penalized (2 min.).

Roughing: Unnecessary roughness (1 or 2 two-min. penalties).

Spearing: Jabbing the blade of the stick into an opponent (5 min.).

Too Many Men: Assessed for having too many men on the ice (2 min.).

Unsportsmanlike Conduct: (2 min.).

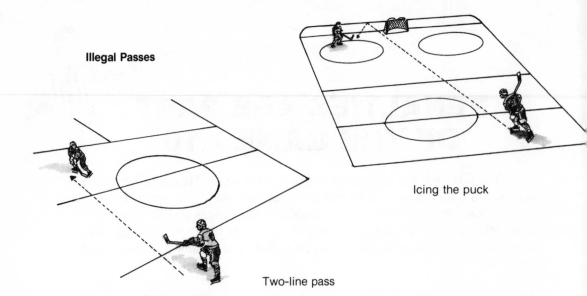

Illegal Passes

Icing the puck

Two-line pass

Hockey as a Contact Sport

Ice hockey is the fastest sport in the world and can be a very violent sport. It has legal body contact at high speeds. There is physical intimidation just as in football. Fighting is presently legal and is punishable only by a two-minute minor penalty or a five-minute major penalty. There is a push to outlaw it, and the present emphasis on speed and offensive play in the NHL has negated some of the more objectionable areas of violence.

Sportsmanship

Hockey has many things to teach. It is a great developer of character. Learning to master the intricacies of the game requires discipline, practice, and learning how to get the best effort out of yourself.

Team play requires coordinating your talents and abilities with those of others. It means following your coach's directions. And it means being in control of yourself.

Is winning important? Of course it is. But is it most important? No. Learning to give your best, learning from your errors, learning from the displayed skills of opponents are all more important than winning one game.

You will be part of a winning team on some days, a losing team on others. When your friends, your teammates, and your opponents call you a good sport, then you really are a winner.

GLOSSARY

Back Check: To check an opponent as close as possible after an offensive rush has failed (legal).

Blue Lines: The pair of one-foot-wide blue lines that extend across the ice at a distance of sixty feet from each goal. These lines divide the ice into attacking, neutral, and defending zones.

Board Check: A body check of an opponent into the boards (illegal).

Body-Check: To hit an opponent with your body in order to take him out of the play (legal).

Breakaway: An offensive rush in which the attacking player breaks into the clear, ahead of all defenders and with a clear path to the goalie, giving him a clear shot on the goalie without any defensive interference.

Butt-End: To jab an opponent with your stick with the end farthest from the blade (illegal).

Center: The centerman in the three-man attacking line.

Center Ice: The neutral area, or no man's land, between the two blue lines.

Center Red Line: The line that divides the ice exactly in half and is the exact center of the rink.

Charge: Charging more than three steps across the ice to body-check an opponent; three steps or more are illegal.

Clear the Puck: To bat or shoot the puck away from the slot area in front of your own goal.

Crease: A four-by-eight box, rectangular in shape, from which attacking players who do not have possession of the puck are forbidden to enter.

Cross-Check: To hit an opponent with both hands on your stick and no part of the stick on the ice in a cross-ways motion (illegal).

Defensemen: The two players whose main job is to assist the goalie in preventing opponent's scores.

Deke: To fake an opponent out of position.

Elbowing: Hitting an opponent violently with your elbow (illegal).

Face-Off: The dropping of a puck between one player from each team in order to start play. It is the hockey equivalent of basketball's jump ball.

Flip Pass: ʌ pass in which the puck is hoisted or lifted in the air so that it may pass over an opponent's stick to a teammate.

Forecheck: To check your opposition in his own defensive end of the rink and prevent him from organizing an offensive rush.

Forwards: The three players who make up an offensive line—the center, left wing, and right wing.

Freeze the Puck: To hold the puck against the boards and create a stoppage of play.

Goal Cage: Sometimes called the net—it is six feet wide and four feet high. The framework, usually made of metal piping, is enclosed with netting to catch the puck when it enters or is shot into the net Most cages are anchored to the ice so they don't move during play.

Goalie: The player, wearing leg pads, who guards the open mouth of the goal cage.

Goal Mouth: The areas just in front of the goal and crease lines.

Hat Trick: The scoring of three or more goals by the same player in a single game.

High-Sticking: Carrying the stick above shoulder level. High-sticking is illegal, particularly if you hit an opponent with the stick above the level of his shoulder.

Holding: Using your hands to hold an opponent (illegal).

Hook Check: A side sweep of the stick close to the ice in an attempt to intercept a pass from an opponent or to intercept an opponent carrying the puck at a certain angle.

Hooking: Using the blade of your stick to grip or hold an opponent, most often from behind (illegal).

Icing the Puck: Intentionally shooting the puck from behind the center red line over your opponent's goal line.

Kicked Goal: A goal intentionally kicked into an opponent's net; it is disallowed. The puck can be propelled on the ice by kicking it, but a legal goal cannot be scored this way.

Major Penalty: A five-minute penalty, usually imposed when the referee rules that there has been an attempt to injure, or blood has been drawn, or there has been a major fight.

Match Misconduct: Any offense that causes a player to be thrown out of the game.

Minor Penalty: A two-minute penalty.

Misconduct Penalty: Ten minutes against an individual player with his team being allowed to substitute for him during the ten minutes.

Off Side: Hockey's basic rule—when an attacking player precedes the puck into the attacking zone, play is halted and restarted with a face-off. Also, when a puck is passed over more than one line and becomes a two-line pass.

Pass Out: A pass by a player on the attack —from either behind the opponent's goal or from the corner to a teammate in front of that goal.

Penalty Box: The area where penalized players serve their time, a small jail.

Penalty Shot: A free shot on goal. The player taking the puck picks up the puck at the center red line, skates in on the goalie unimpeded, and fires a shot on goal. Only the goalkeeper is allowed to attempt to block the shot.

Power Play: A power play occurs when the attacking team has a one or two man advantage because of penalties to the opposition. Normally a coach will use four forwards and one defenseman, employing the extra forward as the point on the blue line, usually a defense position. That forward might be picked because he has an extra hard shot. A coach might use three forwards and two defensemen, but employ two defensemen adept at shooting and passing the puck.

Puck: The vulcanized-rubber disk which is being whacked around the ice. It is frozen for several hours before a game to prevent it from bouncing.

Roughing: A small scale punching or shoving bout (illegal).

Save: A shot blocked by the goaltender.

Shorthanded: Playing with fewer men, either one or two, than your opponent, because of penalties.

Slashing: Swinging your stick violently at an opponent (illegal).

Spearing: Jabbing an opponent with your stick (illegal).

Stickhandle: To control and dribble the puck along the ice.

INDEX